Vancouver is easy to love. Snow-capped mountains frame the skyline, seaplanes skim the harbor and glass towers rise from the edge of the Pacific. It's the image everyone knows. But there's more to the city than what fits on the postcard.

LOST iN takes you inside the studios, kitchens and back alleys where Vancouver's true character takes shape. Meet the photographer documenting women and queer skaters, the artisan sake brewer championing local ingredients, the craft beer icon who set the hazy standard, the rock star making animated punk operas and the Parisian transplant curating one of the city's finest fashion boutiques.

Along the way, join a sunset drum circle on the beach, shoot hoops in a street-art alley, navigate a giant hedge maze, debate the birthplace of the California roll and summon spirits in an occult-themed speakeasy. Then trade the city streets for towering cedars, secret forest trails and mountain views that keep Vancouver's frontier spirit alive.

Culture runs free in a city teetering between glimmering skyscrapers and untamed wilderness. Get lost in Vancouver, where the edge of the wild is your playground.

Pier to Peer

Walk 700 feet into Vancouver Harbour, and the city unfolds around you. The edge of Burrard Dry Dock Pier offers panoramic views of the downtown skyline, the North Shore Mountains and Burrard Inlet before leading back to where Canada built more than a hundred ships for the Allies during World War II. Today, the former shipyard is a lively waterfront plaza with a splash park in summer and an outdoor skating rink in winter.

• Burrard Dry Dock Pier, 15 Wallace Mews, North Vancouver, cnv.org

Photo: Maximilian Rüther

Top Five

Less searching. More doing.

Stanley Park Wildlife Views

- ☐ Prospect Point Lookout
- ☐ Lost Lagoon
- ☐ Beaver Lake
- ☐ Third Beach
- ☐ Ferguson Point

Underrated Beach Days

- ☐ Acadia Beach
- ☐ Ambleside Beach
- ☐ Stearman Beach
- ☐ Wreck Beach
- ☐ Iona Beach

Shopping Streets

- ☐ Main Street (East 7th Ave. to East 33rd Ave.)
- ☐ West 4th Avenue (Vine St. to Pine St.)
- ☐ Robson Street (Hornby St. to Jervis St.)
- ☐ Commercial Drive (Venables St. to East Broadway)
- ☐ Water Street (Richards St. to Carrall St.)

Off-Leash Dog Parks

- ☐ Charleson Dog Park
- ☐ Hadden Beach
- ☐ Spanish Banks Off-Leash
- ☐ Trout Lake Off-Leash Area
- ☐ Coopers' Park

Famous Film Spots

- ☐ Georgia Viaduct (*Deadpool*, 2016)
- ☐ Fairmont Hotel Vancouver (*50 Shades of Grey*, 2015)
- ☐ Eric Hamber Secondary School (*Juno*, 2007)
- ☐ Gastown (*Rumble in the Bronx*, 1995)
- ☐ Thunderbird Stadium (*She's the Man*, 2006)

Live Comedy Venues

- ☐ The Improv Centre
- ☐ Little Mountain Gallery
- ☐ Underground Comedy Club
- ☐ Chill Pill Comedy
- ☐ Comedy After Dark

Waterfront Stays

- ☐ Granville Island Hotel
- ☐ Seaside Hotel North Vancouver
- ☐ Fairmont Waterfront
- ☐ Pan Pacific Vancouver
- ☐ Westin Bayshore

BC Wine Flows

- ☐ Grapes & Soda
- ☐ Is That French
- ☐ The Acorn
- ☐ Bar Tartare
- ☐ La Fabrique St-George

Bike Trails

- ☐ Stanley Park Seawall
- ☐ Arbutus Greenway
- ☐ Seymour Valley Trailway
- ☐ The North Shore Spirit Trail
- ☐ Bobsled/Mount Fromme

Artist Residencies

- ☐ Gibraltar Point Centre for the Arts
- ☐ Open Studio
- ☐ Gladstone House Artist Residency
- ☐ Cedar Ridge Creative Centre
- ☐ The Bentway Artist Residency

Photo: Rhys Abel

Vincent Nguyễn

Family Style

Vincent Nguyễn and Amelie Thuy Nguyễn are siblings, and so are their restaurants. *Anh and Chi,* a modern authentic Vietnamese restaurant, and *Good Thief,* a rebellious, experimental Vietnamese restaurant, stand side by side on Main Street in Mount Pleasant. Each is an award-winning concept in its own right, but paired together, they make an unbeatable evening of dinner and cocktails. The brother-sister duo are second-generation Vietnamese restaurateurs, continuing the legacy of their parents and supporting their community through food and beyond.

Your family has a long history in the Vancouver restaurant industry. How did it begin?

My parents started back in 1983, well before I was born. They actually started selling noodle soup in the backyard of their house until the health inspector came by and said, "Hey, you can't just set up shop in your backyard." So they ended up getting a little shop on Main Street, then moved it to Chinatown, and soon enough, they moved again to Main and 18th.

And that's where Anh and Chi is now?

Yes, the second generation—myself and my sister—took over. We renovated the space completely and built Anh and Chi in the same location where they'd been running their restaurant for 25 years. Now, we're a decade in at Anh and Chi.

Thriving for a decade in the restaurant scene isn't easy. Why do you think Vancouverites love Anh and Chi?

It's something that my parents have always taught us: Just focus on quality and food and people. My parents have been in Mount Pleasant for some time, and when we created Anh and Chi, we didn't want to alienate customers by changing too much. We improved some things, but we kept with tradition, kept the recipes. We remember that this is our community and we want to serve authentic, elevated Vietnamese food. The community is a huge part of who we are.

How do you support and give back to that community?

During the pandemic, we started a program called Reservation by Donation. Our restaurants have been first-come, first-served, and wait times can be an hour, two hours on the weekends. For $10 per person, you can make a reservation and skip the line, and we donate the money to registered charities throughout the Lower Mainland. We've raised over half a million dollars.

You and Amelie's second restaurant, Good Thief, is right next door. How did that come to be?

We love this area. Main Street has grown so much over the years, and we just wanted to continue to add to the community.

Anh and Chi
Mount Pleasant

Good Thief
Mount Pleasant

Sushi Hil
Mount Pleasant

Sumibiyaki Arashi
Mount Pleasant

Published on Main
Mount Pleasant

Dear Gus
Mount Pleasant

What makes Good Thief different from Anh and Chi?

Anh and Chi is an authentic Vietnamese, family-run restaurant. It carries the legacy and the torch of our parents. Good Thief is the sibling. It's rebellious Vietnamese, and the rules don't apply. We're able to push the envelope and bring ingredients and dishes that aren't usually seen.

Can you recommend some dishes from both restaurants?

At Anh and Chi, one specialty that we do is the crispy prawn cakes. They have a burst of coconut flavors, and you wrap them in lettuce. You should also try our spring rolls, which you can find on the Streetside Platter. It's a super-famous and really popular dish, kind of like a deconstructed handroll. Also, the chicken curry and the sablefish. Those are killer, killer dishes. At Good Thief, we have *photine*. It's a pho-flavored brisket with cheese curds and pomme frites, like poutine, that's really fun and delicious. And our signature is our garlic crab noodles with BC Dungeness crab.

What's it like to run a restaurant with your sister?

You know that your sister will always have the best interest for the company, and we always work together to find what's best for our guests and team. That being said, there's no rules. If it's 1am and there's an idea, you're going to call the other person at 1am. There's a lot of passion behind what we do because it is a family-run restaurant, and so it's amazing that we both are able to stay in our own lanes.

What are those lanes?

She's a creative person and very outgoing. She's usually the one doing interviews. I'm a very behind-the-scenes operator, you know. Admin, plumber—you name it, I do it. At

the end of the day, we both want the best for the company and for each other. And don't worry, we still have mom. She's the judge.

What cocktail ingredient do you think is underrated?

Fish sauce. People are like, "Fish sauce, why?" But it brings a lot of umami and salinity to a drink, and balances things out. At Good Thief, there's a pho cocktail we do that proves that.

You've lived in Mount Pleasant all your life. What other restaurants do you recommend?

We've got an amazing sushi restaurant next door called *Sushi Hil*. Get the raw fish. It's delicious. *Sumibiyaki Arashi* is an omakase place that focuses on chicken. They have a Michelin star, and it's delicious as well. Up the road is *Published on Main*, which has great tasting menus and cocktails, and something a bit more cute is *Dear Gus* wine bar. Get the garlic prawns.

What should tourists know about dining in Vancouver?

We are extremely lucky to have such amazing food, but people spend too much time Googling. If you find a place and you enjoy the food, if it's really outstanding, ask the bartender, the manager or the chef where else they go to eat. They're the ones that know what's in town. It's like a secret hack.

What do you like to do when you're not working?

I love to travel. There's so much to learn, so much to eat and drink. I get inspired and bring it back to Vancouver and add it to the restaurants that we have.

Do you have a favorite Vancouver day trip?

There are so many little islands nearby that you can take a quick ferry to. Bowen Island, the Sunshine Coast, Salt Spring Island. You can spend a night or two and get away from all the noise.

Pacific Plates

From just-caught seafood and briny oysters to a world-class Asian food scene that claims the original California roll, Vancouver welcomes you. Now pull up a chair.

Past Perfect

There's really no better place to soak up the city's hipster culture and its fascination with midcentury modern ephemera than at *Mount Pleasant Vintage*. Part vintage shop, part coolest bar in town, the room is lively and, frankly, next to impossible to get into on a weekend. Some of this is because of the patios—two of the best in the city—and some of it is the vibe inside. It's a little bit like hanging out in your grandma's living room, if your whole family's been replaced by a hundred tattooed strangers, and instead of Elvis Presley on the stereo, it's Biggie.

• Mount Pleasant Vintage & Provisions, 67 West 6th Avenue, Mount Pleasant, mtpleasant.bar

La Dolce Vita

It's hard to believe the ultra-chic *Elio Volpe* was once a mechanic shop. This Italian osteria, with its showstopping central bar, warm lighting and even warmer wood-fired pizza oven, has been a smash hit since opening in 2024. The evening menu highlights include Calabreselli alla vodka with whipped ricotta and hot-honey *pepperone* pizza. For weekend brunch, there's brioche French toast, lobster Benedict and more pizza, which you can top with a poached egg. *Savio Volpe*, its big sister restaurant in nearby Fraserhood, is absolutely worth a visit as well.

• Osteria Elio Volpe, 540 West 17th Avenue, Cambie Village, eliovolpe.com

Wait for It

Asian cuisine is the beating heart of the food scene, and there's a mind-boggling selection to choose from. This family-run Cambodian restaurant consistently tops lists for its extensive menu of more than a hundred rice, noodle and soup dishes. The classics are what keep this place busy, and "busy" means "prepare to wait at least a half hour, any time of day, for a table." The holy trinity of *Phnom Penh* is the butter beef, beef luc lac with an egg and, most famous of all, the chicken wings, which are an institution unto themselves.

• Phnom Penh, 244 East Georgia Street, Chinatown, @phnompenh.restaurant

Bet the Farm

Farmer's Apprentice blends farm-to-fork philosophy with global cuisine, and even the staff struggles to define it. The menu shifts constantly based on what's local, in season and inspiring the kitchen staff that week. French, Mexican, Indian, Middle Eastern and other influences mingle, sometimes in the same dish. Signature cocktails are mixed and bottled next door at sister bar *Grapes & Soda* for additional artisanal polish, and the selection changes frequently. The room itself seats just 30 people, farmhouse-cozy, with a full view into the open kitchen as the cooks prepare your meal.

• Farmer's Apprentice, 1535 West 6th Avenue, South Granville, farmersapprentice.ca

Market Moves

Vancouverites tend to avoid the traffic of the traditional tourist destinations, but *Granville Island Public Market* is a bustling, beautiful exception. You're just as likely to find visitors gawking at a spread of fresh pastries as you are locals picking up their favorite honey mustard pickles. With more than 50 local vendors, there's fresh fish, local produce, baked goods, artisanal cheeses, jewelry, clothing and more. On sunny days, it's best practice to grab food and sit oceanside for views of the tiny ferry boats. Just watch out for seagulls: They are both hungry and fearless.

• Granville Island Public Market, 1689 Johnston Street, Granville Island, granvilleisland.com

The Devil You Know

Dive bar culture has mostly been erased from the downtown scene, but the vestiges of that old-school grit can still be felt in the brick-walled *Devil's Elbow*. Rowdy and down-home, the space feels like New York City, while the food is straight Southern barbecue. Load up on shared platters of smoked beef brisket, pulled pork or fall-off-the-bone pork ribs while sipping on a well-rounded lineup of the best local craft beers the city can offer. Its location near Rogers Arena and BC Place makes it an ideal pre-game and post-show hangout.

• Devil's Elbow Ale & Smokehouse, 562 Beatty Street, Crosstown, devilselbowalehouse.com

A Royal Affair

For inventive dishes in a laid-back setting, chef Angus An's *Maenam* is the reservation to make. An's modern Thai cooking has earned him local and international awards, including a Michelin guide listing. The crispy banana blossom and pomelo salad and the pad thai made from fresh rice noodles are consistent crowd-pleasers, but if you really want to dig into the kitchen's latest creations and seasonal West Coast ingredients, it's best to go with the multicourse, family-style chef's menu. Ask your server for recommended wine pairings from the well-curated bar to elevate the experience further.

• Maenam, 1938 West 4th Avenue, Kitsilano, maenam.ca

Honor Roll

They say history is written by the winners, and the history of sushi is no exception. That a roll made with crab, avocado and cucumber, encased in nori and surrounded by seasoned rice, is known as a California roll is proof of that.

Los Angeles chef Ichiro Mashita is often credited with creating this popular Western roll, but the original inventor is still debated today. A legion of fans and supporters believe that chef Hidekazu Tojo—an award-winning, Vancouver-based Japanese restaurateur who opened his eponymous restaurant in Vancouver in 1988—is the true California king.

If you ask Chef Tojo, he'll tell you he created his inside-out Tojo roll to appeal to Vancouver diners in the 1980s, as the majority of his guests had rarely if ever had sushi. He used fully cooked crab in place of raw fish and hid the nori inside the rice to convince his patrons that the dish was worth a try. It totally worked. Worth noting, one origin story suggests the California roll started out as the "C.A. roll," with the initials standing for crab and avocado.

We'll probably never know whether Tojo's inside-out roll or Mashita's California roll came first, or if they were dreamed up at the same time by two like-minded strangers, but the impact of Tojo's cooking on Vancouver cannot be overstated. His decades of devoted service to the city helped pave the way for other iconic chefs, such as the Michelin-starred Masayoshi Baba, and made Japanese food a true staple of the local food scene.

There's no need to skip raw fish or disguise nori when eating out in this city, however. Vancouver is recognized as one of the best places to get sushi outside of Japan.

Flying High

The playful pan-Asian plates at *PiDGiN* practically scream "no rules in the kitchen." Expect mad fusion like kimchi croquettes and chewy Korean rice cakes tossed in gochujang Bolognese. Opt for the tasting menu (vegetarian available) or order à la carte alongside drink options like sake, cider and natural wine. The only hesitation for some visitors is the location. *PiDGiN*, along with nearby Japanese-Italian standout *Kissa Tanto*, sits on the edge of Downtown Eastside (DTES), a gritty area where visible drug use can be a culture shock. Taking a taxi or rideshare is advised.

• PiDGiN, 350 Carrall Street, Gastown, pidginvancouver.com

Shuck Yeah

BC Oyster Primer

You don't need a map to tell you Vancouver is a seaside city. Just open a menu. Fresh seafood—from wild salmon and albacore tuna to Dungeness crab, spot prawns and plump mussels—is everywhere, but the coast's most beloved delicacy is the oyster.

British Columbia is Canada's largest producer of farmed oysters, thanks to its cold, nutrient-rich waters and productive intertidal coastline. The province farms an impressive variety of oysters, each with its own personality. Olympia oysters, the only species native to the Pacific coast, are small, intensely briny and peppery. Pacific oysters, introduced from Japan in the early 20th century, are prized for their crisp texture and subtle cucumber finish. The locally developed Royal Miyagi, a cultivated variety of the Pacific oyster, is known for its creamy texture and balanced sweetness, while European flats offer a bold, mineral-rich flavor often described as coppery.

Behind every shell is a careful balancing act. Oyster farmers raise their crop using floating cages, suspended rafts, longlines and intertidal beach farms, adapting their methods to tides, currents and the surrounding marine ecosystem. It's patient work that often takes two to three years before an oyster is ready for the plate.

Oyster aficionados often talk about "merroir," the marine equivalent of terroir, as every bay and inlet produces oysters with subtly different flavors. For this reason, oysters are often named after the waters in which they're grown, such as Fanny Bay, Kusshi and Sawmill Bay. Most oysters served in Vancouver are harvested along the sheltered coastlines of Vancouver Island, the Sunshine Coast and the Discovery Islands, arriving at restaurants within hours.

Whether topped with caviar, drizzled with truffle or herb butter, or served simply on the half shell with lemon, horseradish and mignonette, Vancouver's oysters prove that sometimes the smallest things on the menu make the biggest impression.

The Raw Truth

BC is famous for its seafood, and one of the best places to sample the finest regional fish and shellfish is *Coast*. Located in an exclusive area of downtown, it's a true seafood lover's paradise. Seafood towers? Check. Sushi plates with pristine salmon? Absolutely. The vibe is pure West Coast, from the lobster tails chilling on ice behind the bar to the beachside artwork on the walls. It also boasts one of the best happy hours in town, complete with its famous deep-fried lobster mac and cheese bites. Don't skip 'em.

• Coast, 1054 Alberni Street, Downtown, glowbalgroup.com/coast

Shell Game

When in oyster country, there's arguably no better place to hunker down and shuck a few dozen than *Rodney's*. A local institution since 1998, it's as renowned for its exceptional selection of oysters as it is for its rowdy East Coast party atmosphere. The menu showcases some of the best oysters from BC's shores alongside imports from Atlantic Canada, Ireland and New Zealand. Each platter comes with a variety of sauces ranging from mild to eye-watering.

• Rodney's Oyster House, 1228 Hamilton Street, Yaletown, rohvan.com

Briny Bay

Shuck, slurp, repeat. It's the mantra at *Fanny Bay Oysters*, emblazoned on the T-shirts of several staff and a concise indicator of what's in store. The menu boasts every kind of locally sourced seafood imaginable, from sea urchin sashimi to salmon caviar, but it's the oysters that are worth the trip. The restaurant is the retail outpost of a family-run oyster farm that has harvested shellfish in the Strait of Georgia for more than 40 years. SunSeeker is kelpy and sweet, while the namesake Fanny Bay is crisp, cucumbery and famously gigantic. You can also pick up fresh or frozen shellfish to enjoy at home.

• Fanny Bay Oyster Bar & Shellfish Market, 762 Cambie Street, Downtown, fannybayoysters.com

Masa Shiroki

Field of Dreams

In 2007, Masa and Yukiko Shiroki launched their own sake business, and in 2015, bottled the first craft sake made from 100 percent Canadian-grown rice. Using equipment, rice varieties and expertise imported from Japan, they created their Osake line of artisan sakes to introduce Canadians to the world of rice wine. At their Granville Island shop and tasting room, *Artisan SakeMaker*, visitors from around the world can sample and learn about the centuries-old beverage. Next door, *Sake & Tapas* pairs their sake with Japanese small plates like chicken karaage, shishito peppers and dried sardines.

You don't come from a family of brewers or sakemakers. How were you introduced to the alcohol production industry?

During my tenure with the BC government, I was hired as a desk officer for Japan Trade and Investment. There was an export opportunity for craft beer brewing systems made in Canada. In Japan, craft beer making was very new, and the government wanted to explore opportunities to start up a new industry. This is where it started, although it has nothing to do with sake.

How did this lead to sake?

The contacts. Not only with the BC suppliers, but also with Japanese buyers and Japanese sakemakers. It was such a nice full-circle development. I met with those people because I wanted to help, and now I'm talking about starting my own business in sakemaking. So I asked: Where do I find equipment? Where do I find seeds? Where do I find the technical expertise? And so forth.

What was the answer?

Hokkaido, in a place called Rumoi. That's where I eventually brought in everything from Japan.

Tell us about your decision to start making sake when your government service ended.

I started my new second life at the age of 50 to venture into something that I had never done before. At that time, I made two promises to myself. One, I am going to represent our culture, Japanese culture, and influence people's mindset about sake. Two, I was committed to starting my own rice production venture.

You produce your sake from your rice paddy in Abbotsford, a city about 43 miles from Vancouver. Do most Japanese sakemakers farm their own rice?

In Japan, very few sakemakers would even consider growing their own rice. Because that's the system: The rice production relies on the farmers. I researched BC's climatic patterns in a variety of places, especially the hot spots, including Kamloops, Ashcroft, Peachland, Agassiz, Cowichan Bay and Abbotsford. I also made a trip to Japan specifically to source the type of rice seeds that may succeed in this climate. I chose to start my own farm in Abbotsford, taking the same kind of path that the winemakers in the Okanagan would have taken.

How is sake made?

Sake is a rice wine, so it goes through a fermentation process. We use rice as our main ingredient, but we also need what we call *koji*, which is similar to yeast. It has an enzyme that has the power to break down starch into sugar. With that sugar, yeast can thrive, multiply and start producing alcohol. Changing the proportions of rice, koji and water will affect the outcome: sweetness, strength and how it pairs with food.

Your sake shop is on Granville Island, one of the busiest tourist spots in the city. Why do you like working there?

It's international. Lots of curious minds are gathered on Granville Island, especially in the row where we are located. It's a mixture of young people hustling and older, retired people who have lots of exposure to foreign cultures. It's a communal sort of atmosphere.

As the first sakemaker of your kind in Canada, how did you make your product accessible to Canadians who might have limited experience with it?

I wanted to come up with a style of sake that would be more acceptable to the Canadian palate. The bottle looks like a wine bottle, and I studied wine beforehand. This helped me to understand what kind of flavors, aromas and pairing possibilities Canadians would be looking for.

Which sake should visitors try first?

We have a very adaptable, approachable sake called Junmai Nama. Junmai means "pure rice," which means our style of making sake does not involve the addition of distilled alcohol. Adding distilled alcohol makes the sake drier, but our style brings out the umami factor, which is the savory nature or characteristics of the drink, as much as we can.

What pairings would you suggest?

I would say Junmai Nama and oysters. Because oysters have a lot of umami factors, and the brine, the saltiness of oyster, brings out the sweetness of sake. Another one is Junmai Genshu with blue cheese, especially the blue cheese that is available at *Benton Brothers [Fine Cheese]* on Granville Island. Because Junmai Genshu has a higher alcohol level of 18 percent, it can stand up to a lot of Western food, especially rich cheese.

Oyama Sausage
Granville Island

Granville Island Hotel
Granville Island

Sandbar Restaurant
Granville Island

Kishimoto
Grandview-Woodland

The Acorn
Riley Park

Where else should tourists shop on Granville Island?

Oyama Sausage. We have collaborative production of one item there, the Kazu Coppa. The pork meat is cured in sake kasu for three months and produces a wonderful prosciutto-like product.

What part of Granville Island is the most underrated?

The patio at the back of the *Granville Island Hotel*. It oversees the entire False Creek community. Unfortunately, people don't usually go there. People always go to the market, which can be like being in a washing machine. But you can have peace of mind on that patio.

What are your favorite Japanese restaurants in the city?

For something relatively affordable, the sushi counter on the second floor of *Sandbar Restaurant* has an assortment of sushi and satisfies you completely. For fancier food, I would go to *Kishimoto* on Commercial Drive. The chef [Akira Kishimoto] is a kaiseki chef from Kyoto, so seasonality is the key for him.

Any other spots to recommend for dining?

A very creative vegan place is *The Acorn* restaurant. They have dishes that go with sake. That is the reason why I like to recommend them, because they understand the sake very well.

Rain City Pours

Beyond the standard watering hole lies Vancouver's true liquid geography. Discover the hidden spaces, curation and character defining the city's nightlife.

Bars with Benefits

Vancouver is overflowing with places to grab a drink, from laid-back patios to sexy late-night haunts. In a city spoiled for choice, some bars stand out by offering something beyond beer, wine and cocktails: a built-in activity to break the ice and keep the conversation flowing.

At Gastown's *Back and Forth Bar,* that activity is table tennis, with six ping-pong tables available to rent by the hour. Just five minutes away, *Greta Bar* pairs more than 50 arcade games—including *Mario Kart, Guitar Hero* and *Pac-Man*—with elevated pub fare like Jamaican patty spring rolls, birria tacos and burrata pasta. Downtown's *Par-Tee Putt* serves cocktails alongside 24 themed mini-golf holes, many inspired by Vancouver landmarks. Over in Kitsilano, *Charqui* hosts karaoke every night—yes, every single night—while the *American* on Main Street keeps things lively with pinball, pool and a vintage photo booth.

At all of the above, the drinks and the conversation never go dry.

• Various locations

Liquid Apothecary

Picture a cocktail bar in *Blade Runner*, and you'll have an idea of what awaits at the *Keefer Bar*. Inspired by historic Chinese pharmacies, this intimate, windowless space seats fewer than 50 beneath a moody glow of deep red lights. The cinematic atmosphere is only the beginning. For more than a decade, the bar has been at the forefront of Vancouver's cocktail scene, pairing meticulous mixology with inventive drinks infused with herbs, spices and other apothecary-inspired ingredients.

• The Keefer Bar, 135 Keefer Street, Chinatown, thekeeferbar.com

The Rabbit Hole

Before you even step inside *Prophecy*, you know something mysterious is afoot. A bunny with angel wings marks the entrance. Beyond the cast-iron doors, a mirrored hallway descends into what feels like a subterranean vampire lounge—albeit one with A Tribe Called Quest on the speakers. Dark corners, candlelight and heavy velvet curtains keep the intrigue alive, while inventive cocktails and live funk, soul, jazz and dance music make it all too easy to lose track of time in this windowless hideaway.

• Prophecy Bar, 801 West Georgia Street, Downtown, prophecybar.com

That '70s Pour

Get out of your cocktail comfort zone with *Meo*. Plush velvety booths, a glowing jukebox and a rosy interior bring 1970s living-room vibes to a bar with bold cocktails. Signature drinks range from a matcha highball with banana milk to a dirty lychee martini, and seasonal offerings might include ingredients like prickly pear, chocolate mint and green apricot chutney. No matter the season, the bartenders always explore ways to incorporate the atypical. The food menu is equally inspired, with choices like curried potato milk buns and scallop crudo with passionfruit and corn emulsion.

• Meo, 265 East Pender Street, Chinatown, meochinatown.com

Gin & Sonic

Listening bars have finally taken off in Vancouver, and there's no better space to combine architectural groove with impeccable sound design than *Lala*. Located underneath *June on Cambie*—itself a stellar dining experience—the Lala basement bar is expansive, classy and futuristic. The vinyl selectors spin a mix of electronic, jazz, classic rock and classic pop. It's a small and intimate space with excellent cocktails. And the sound? The best. Clear enough even at low volumes to hear every note, clean enough when the music is booming to hear your partner speak.

• Lala, 3305 Cambie Street, Cambie Village, juneoncambie.com

Earth & Wine

Vancouver is about as West Coast as it gets, but that doesn't mean you can't find a little slice of Old World Europe. Tucked into the Brewery Creek neighborhood of Mount Pleasant, *La Fabrique* makes its wines on-site using traditional clay amphorae known as *qvevri*. The earthen vessels are the first thing you'll notice as you step inside the warm, rustic tasting lounge. The wine list ranges from crisp sparkling whites to bold Syrahs, alongside a thoughtful selection of natural wines from across British Columbia.

• La Fabrique St. George, 7 East 7th Avenue, Mount Pleasant, fabriquestgeorge.com

The Prohibition Boom

Raise a glass to the city's spirited past.

The experiment was short-lived. After going dry in 1917, British Columbia repealed Prohibition just four years later. Public bars remained closed until 1925, but new beer parlor licenses allowed hotels to serve beer by the glass once again. Vancouver's saloons were back and perfectly timed to welcome American visitors, whose own Prohibition era was only just beginning.

For the rest of the decade, BC sold legal, government-regulated booze while the States languished in the dry zone. Vancouver became a destination for Americans in search of a drink and a major launch point for rum-runners smuggling Canadian liquor south. The most famous was Victoria's Johnny Schnarr, who claimed to have made 400 cross-border runs without ever being caught. But he was far from alone.

These smugglers loaded cases of Canadian whisky onto large schooners in Burrard Inlet before slipping into international waters to rendezvous with American buyers. Among them was the *Malahat*, a five-masted Vancouver schooner so notorious along the California coast that sailors dubbed her the Queen of Rum Row. Others relied on speedboats powered by surplus First World War aircraft engines, threading through narrow island channels under the cover of darkness while outrunning Coast Guard cutters armed with machine guns.

When the United States finally repealed Prohibition, Vancouver's decade-long booze boom began to fade. Not that the city's drinking culture was especially wild to begin with. The beer parlors that opened in 1925 were so tightly regulated that food, entertainment, standing and even dancing were prohibited. So while Americans crossed the border in search of legal hooch, they found themselves drinking in highly regulated surroundings.

A handful of Vancouver bars from that era are still pouring drinks today, and they're considerably livelier now. *Ivanhoe Pub* is a true dive bar, valued as much for its history as its cheap drinks. Located near the railyards and beside Hogan's Alley, the heart of Vancouver's Black community and jazz scene, it became a gathering place for transient workers, sailors and bootleggers moving liquor down the coast.

The Lamplighter Public House (photo) occupies the ground floor of Gastown's historic Dominion Hotel, where BC's first beer parlor license—License No. 1—was issued on March 20, 1925. The hotel paid $750 for the privilege. It was also among the city's first bars to admit women, making it a popular stop for passengers stepping off the steamships in search of a legal drink. Today, it's a popular hangout, centrally located and stocked with pinball machines, arcade games and a bustling crowd.

A few blocks away, the *Cambie* has anchored the same Gastown corner since the 1890s, operating under several names over the years. During Prohibition, it housed a cabaret where bootleggers reportedly moved cases of liquor through an underground tunnel from the storeroom to rum-runner boats bound for the United States. Today, it's one of the city's last great dive bars, serving affordable drinks to a loyal mix of travelers, exchange students and locals.

Further south in the downtown core, the *Hotel Georgia* opened in 1927 at the height of Vancouver's Prohibition-era boom. It quickly became ground zero for high society, welcoming Edward, Prince of Wales, and later a parade of Hollywood royalty, including Frank Sinatra and Katharine Hepburn. Eventually gutted and restored as the *Rosewood Hotel Georgia*, the landmark now pays tribute to its Jazz Age roots with the elegant *1927 Lounge* (photo above). It remains one of the city's most atmospheric spots to sip a classic Prohibition-era cocktail.

Speakeasies

Under Cover

Step through the hidden door and into another world.

The Dumpling Says "Shh"

You think you're only ordering dumplings. And you can do that. *Blnd Tger's* offerings are a true blend of Old World flavor and New World flair. Order the secret recipe, however, and the front-of-house staff grants access to *Laowai*, the cocktail bar behind a wall. The room is a testament to Vancouver's flourishing Chinese culture and to how far it has come since Chinatown was first founded as a blue-collar neighborhood. But it's the cocktails that sell this place. They're as creative and exotic as you're likely to find anywhere in this city.

• Laowai, 251 East Georgia Street, Chinatown, laowai.ca

The Winning Ticket

There's no address, just newspaper-covered windows. Inside is a horse-betting parlor, but don't be fooled: Pick the right horse, and a hidden door opens to a room straight out of a Rudyard Kipling novel. Portraits of British Indian imperialists, brass monkey sculptures and period curios line the tunnel-shaped walls. The cocktails lean on gin and bold flavors, the menu arrives as a beautifully illustrated children's book, and the food draws inspiration from the city's Indian heritage. If the time warp feels a little too convincing, the DJ's electro-funk soundtrack keeps you grounded.

• Bagheera Bar, 518 Main Street, Chinatown, bagheera.bar

Hidden Shame

From the outside, it's another day on Main Street. Inside, you're in an all-encompassing Polynesian nightclub, complete with tiki decor and no natural light. *The Shameful Tiki* is one of the city's most popular hidden gems and nearly impossible to get into without a reservation. Some of this is the vibe. Some of it is the drinks—zany Pacific island concoctions that come in enormous vessels best shared. And some is the entertainment: intentionally kitsch lounge acts that transport you directly to some off-the-Vegas-strip hotel lounge where dreams go to die. But there's nothing macabre about this tiki bar. It's a hothouse of good times. Just beware the Mystery Bowl.

• The Shameful Tiki Room, 4362 Main Street, Riley Park, shamefultikiroom.com

The Witching Hour

The occult is alive and well in this nondescript corner of Gastown. Outside, you're invited into a pet psychic parlor, but as you walk through the entry of *Arcana Spirit Lounge*, it's as if you've arrived at Aleister Crowley's private bar, where "spirit" takes on a double meaning. The room is a portal, complete with three-dimensional hologram skulls and melted candle wax piling up. The cocktails offer a mix of the classics and concoctions bordering on the mystical (yes, these bartenders like absinthe). The occultist flair doesn't stop there: Even the burger buns are branded with pentagrams.

• Arcana Spirit Lounge, 238 Abbott Street, Gastown, arcanabar.com

SUPERFLUX

Adam Henderson

Hazy Days

East Vancouver's *Superflux Beer Company* is an award-winning brewery known for bold flavors, beautiful graphic design and a dog-friendly patio. It also happens to serve hot dogs piled with creative toppings like sautéed oyster mushrooms and mac and cheese. Founded in 2015 by Adam Henderson (photo right) and Matt Kohlen (left), two buddies with a taste for hops, the brewery is a local favorite for hazy IPAs.

How did you and Matt first meet?

Matt and I met at a bar in Kitsilano that he was working at, the *Local [Public Eatery]*. I was a beer vendor of theirs. We ended up connecting and talking about beer. We had the same dream. We started our project in 2015, brewing beer together after talking about it for a long time.

How do you even start a brewery?

We started at [now closed] Callister Brewing, a brewery incubator. We made some beer there under the name Machine Ale for about a year and then started Superflux. We bounced around a little bit, did some contract brewing at *Dogwood Brewing* and *Strathcona Brewing*, and then opened our own place in August of 2020. Matt's departed the company now, but he was both a bartender and a kind of digital entrepreneur with great graphic design skills. He did a lot of our design, including our current flagship labels. He's a very talented guy.

Superflux is best known for IPAs, or India Pale Ales. What made you want to focus on this kind of beer?

When we were at Callister, we weren't sure what kind of beers were going to resonate with the market, but we always felt there was more opportunity for IPAs. And then once we started making them, we realized our approach had a great fit, and we quickly stopped making anything else. IPA has always been the biggest style of craft beer in North America, and actually, even in Europe today. It moves the needle. People want to come in and drink it. Also, Matt experimented with the first hazy IPA I ever had.

What makes a hazy IPA different from a regular IPA?

Other than the obvious, which is that it's pretty opaque, the first thing that makes it different in general is the process of creating it makes the hop character more fruit-forward. It isn't as bitter as the hoppy beers from 15 to 20 years ago. The second thing is it's designed to keep that haze in suspension. For lack of a scientific term, the yeast and the hops are kind of high-fiving, and the hop oils keep some of the yeast in suspension.

What does that high five do to the beer?

It allows some of the more interesting hop oils to come through, which aromatically express themselves like citrus and sometimes candy or blueberry. Sometimes there's crazier flavors like diesel but in a very pleasant way.

What Superflux beer would you recommend to an IPA amateur?

Colour & Shape, our flagship IPA. Without sounding like a cop-out, it's great for beginners

Superflux Beer Company
Strathcona

Local Public Eatery
Kitsilano, Gastown, Kamloops, Penticton, River District

Dogwood Brewing
Sunset

Strathcona Brewing
Downtown Eastside

Luppolo Brewing
Strathcona

Parallel 49
East Vancouver

Threefold Brewery
East Vancouver

Kitsilano Beach
Kitsilano

Woodland Park
Grandview-Woodland

and for people who love IPAs. It's like a movie for film buffs that normal people could watch, too. It's one of our enduring successes.

Your brewery, designed by local architect Bill Uhrich of Table Architectural Collective, has been featured in local magazines. Why was beautiful brewery design important to you?

We're on one of the busiest industrial streets in Western Canada, so there's trucks, it's loud, it's full of brake dust. We wanted to use the space we had to get people off of that street and pull you into the brewery. So, the tasting room is in the heart of the building, and that allowed us to create a more immersive space.

Tell us about the space itself.

You're sitting amongst the brewery. There's no illusion that you're not in a brewery. We found a lot of inspiration in cleaner surfaces: concrete and natural wood and white, but with some cool textural elements that keep it interesting and give some movement. It's a pretty cool thing to have accomplished in a giant square cinder-block building.

If a tourist stops by Superflux and wants to go on a self-guided beer crawl, what other breweries in the neighborhood should they visit?

We are positioned where mostly all of the breweries are in East Vancouver. *Strathcona Brewing*, where we started, is a great place to go. *Luppolo [Brewing]* is great for lagers, and they also have great pizza. *Parallel 49* has a big patio. *Threefold Brewery* is a really cool spot. It has three different breweries under one roof: *Temporal*, *Slow Hand* and *Boombox*.

Vancouver has many alcohol-friendly beaches and parks. Where is your favorite place to crack open a beer on a sunny day?

I live near *Kitsilano Beach*, and that's a good spot for sure. *Woodland Park* is also very close to the brewery and a popular place for our fans.

Kin Kao Thai Kitchen
Grandview-Woodland

Mon Pitou
Fairview

JJ Bean
Granville Island

Elysian
Kitsilano, Mount Pleasant, Fairview, Downtown

Pepino's Spaghetti House
Grandview-Woodland

Downlow Chicken Shack
East Vancouver, UBC, Kitsilano

Give us a beer and takeout recommendation.

Kin Kao [Thai Kitchen] is a great place, and Thai food with our Colour & Shape IPA is really awesome.

Say it's too early for a beer. Any go-to coffee shops?

I like a cute little spot called *Mon Pitou*. And I think I first learned about *JJ Bean* at Granville Island Market, which is not a fun place to drive a car to, but I love living by it. I like *Elysian* as well. It's a great place to go and get a cup of coffee.

Any other favorite neighborhood spots?

We're very close to Commercial Drive. *Pepino's Spaghetti House* and *Downlow Chicken Shack* are really great options.

Outside of work, what outdoor activities do you get up to?

I golf often, which is nice and works well with a beer. We like to run with our husky, Shiloh. And I try to ski as much as I can.

What's a popular tourist spot that you like to visit yourself?

You can't miss the seawall, and it almost doesn't matter what time of year it is. It's a pretty epic feature of Vancouver, and there's lots of good spots to go for a long bike ride, walk or hike. I don't think I ever take that for granted.

The Craft Coast

For a while, the city's craft beer industry was the most authentic cultural experience it had to offer. The city's music venues were shutting down, the restaurant scene hadn't yet taken off, and the breweries filled the void. What resulted is a brewery culture dominated by experimentation and creativity, with tasting rooms that promote dependable good times, serving up the best vibes—and yes, beer—possible. Since the scene exploded in 2014, Vancouver's brewery culture has been recognized worldwide, with its breweries winning national and international beer competitions on the regular.

Three's Company

The latest addition to the craft beer scene is actually three breweries in one. There's *Slow Hand Beer Company*, which specializes in lagers and pilsners; *Boombox Brewing*, which covers the hazy IPAs; and *Temporal Artisan Ales*, for anyone seeking barrel-aged sours or more refined, experimental brews. Between the three, they offer some of the best versions in their respective categories, in a room that's built out like your parents' basement from the 1980s. And there's some excellent Neapolitan pizza to boot.

• Threefold Beer, 1507 Powell Street, East Vancouver, threefoldbeer.com

Brass Appeal

Imagine a cozy little room where everyone knows your name, or, if they don't already, they very well could. It's a room where the beer is experimental and approachable and provides the necessary kind of social lubricant needed to form a strong bond with the person next to you, even if only for the evening. That describes *Brassneck*—a hallmark and standard bearer of the city's vibrant craft beer movement—to a T. The menu changes regularly, but expect a bit of everything, from West Coast IPAs to a traditional Bavarian wheat beer to a chocolate banana Imperial Milkshake Stout. And quite literally everything in between.

• Brassneck Brewery, 2148 Main Street, Mount Pleasant, brassneck.ca

The First Pour

The one that started it all. At least in Vancouver. *Parallel 49* opened in 2012 with a tiny, dingy tasting room that felt, somehow, like the monkeys had taken over the zoo. Since then, P49 has expanded and evolved into one of the liveliest tasting rooms anywhere in British Columbia, with a beer menu defined as much by its restless experimentation as by its reliable staples. The on-site food menu is an elevated food-truck experience: It's quite literally made inside a food truck built into the tasting room. Great patio, too.

• Parallel 49 Brewing Company, 1950 Triumph Street, Hastings Sunrise, parallel49brewing.com

Less Is More

The epitome of craft beer cool, *33 Acres* is in some ways the antithesis of what defines so many other breweries. Where others revel in experimentation and regular releases, 33A defines itself with a smaller menu of carefully considered beers that are delicious and dependable. The brewery itself is among the most popular spots in the city, and any weekend evening is crammed wall-to-wall with the city's grooviest youth. But if you do want more small-batch experimentation, head next door to *33 Brewing Experiment*, better known as 33B. Different room, weirder beers, same vibe.

• 33 Acres Brewing Company, 15 West 8th Avenue, Mount Pleasant, 33acresbrewing.com

Outdoors

Call of the Wild

Skip the gym. Go paddleboarding. Or hiking. Or swimming. Around here, the outdoors are everyone's favorite pastime.

Chasing Sunsets

Vancouver's divergent personality traits feed its dynamic character, and its sunset rituals are essential in that. At Kits Beach, the volleyball games run past sunset, players silhouetted against North Shore mountains turning pink. Out in False Creek, beer drinkers, tallboys in hand, colonize the rocks of Habitat Island—better known as Beer Island—as the light fades over downtown across the water. Down at clothing-optional Wreck Beach, the day's revelers send up a howl as the sun dips behind the Gulf Islands way across the Salish Sea. And almost everyone else who's out and about simply claims a patio and orders another round as the sky darkens.

• Various locations

High Point

Queen Elizabeth Park, the highest point in Vancouver proper, shines with bright floral gardens, tall evergreen trees and, in the springtime, a snow-like parade of soft pink cherry blossom petals. The *Bloedel Conservatory*, a dome-shaped tropical indoor oasis with exotic birds, is right in the park's center. If taking in the abundant splendors of our natural world isn't enough, you'll also find an upscale restaurant, lots of recreational space and everything from basketball and pickleball courts to a disc golf and regular golf course. There's even a baseball stadium across the street.

- Queen Elizabeth Park, 4600 Cambie Street, Riley Park, vancouver.ca

The Easy Way Up

Psst: You don't have to devote an entire day to climbing a mountain to get a panoramic view. *Quarry Rock*, an amateur adventurer's destination in Deep Cove on the North Shore, is the kind of part-walk, part-hike activity that many choose to do in sandals. This isn't recommended, of course, but it's true. Getting up and down takes about two hours, and the elevation gain is a little more than 300 feet, but the lookout on the modest summit offers an incredible landscape of ocean, mountains, forest and city. The earlier in the morning you hit this hike, the better, as it's a popular one.

- Quarry Rock Hike, 2400 Panorama Drive, Deep Cove, deepcovebc.ca

A Shore Thing

Vancouver is famous for its coastline, but which beach is best? The city has no shortage of contenders.

English Bay is the postcard classic, stretching along the edge of downtown with views of the North Shore mountains. It's also the most crowded. A 15-minute bike ride along the seawall brings you to Third Beach, where the views are similar but the crowds thin out and the atmosphere transitions to a more laid-back party vibe. West of downtown, Kitsilano Beach—or simply Kits—is a local favorite, with beach volleyball courts, a large saltwater pool and plenty of room to spread out. Farther west, Spanish Banks is famous for its dramatic low tides, which reveal vast sand flats perfect for long walks. Then there's Wreck Beach, Canada's largest nude beach and a lasting reminder of the city's hippie roots.

Still, the beaches aren't just for swimming and sunbathing. Summer evenings often bring the sound of hand drums echoing across the sand. Since the mid-2000s, Brahm's Tams Drum Circle has drawn drummers, dancers, fire spinners, hula hoopers and sunset watchers to Third Beach every Tuesday, becoming one of the city's most beloved summer traditions. The longest-running gathering, however, takes place on Sunday evenings at Spanish Banks, where drummers have been keeping the beat since 1979.

Whether you're surfing, drumming or simply watching the sun disappear behind the mountains, Vancouver's beaches are where the city slows down when the sun comes out.

• Various locations

Vancouver Untamed

You're sipping an espresso with high-rises all around when a heron flaps past at eye level. That's Vancouver. *Stanley Park* (left) holds one of North America's largest heron colonies, while harbor seals bob through the kelp off nearby English Bay. So do whales, in fact: Orcas now patrol local waters roughly 250 days a year, with humpbacks and grey whales joining in from time to time. Eagles are as common as Teslas in nearby Squamish and Tsawwassen, if you're willing to drive. You can also watch salmon battle their way upriver at the Capilano hatchery every October, and, if you're lucky, you might see a black bear wander down for a snack while you're there. In Vancouver, the line between city and wilderness is beautifully blurred.

• Various locations

In Full Bloom

Every spring, the city bursts into shades of pink as more than 40,000 cherry trees come into bloom, transforming streets, parks and waterfront paths into one of the city's most photogenic spectacles. Timed with the blossoms, the *Vancouver Cherry Blossom Festival* celebrates spring through guided walks, pop-up performances, picnics and community events across the city. While favorites like *Stanley Park* and Queen Elizabeth Park draw the biggest crowds, some of the most rewarding displays are found along quiet residential streets. Bloom times vary each year, but late March through April is typically the sweet spot.

• Vancouver Cherry Blossom Festival, vcbf.ca

North Shore Rides

Ask any mountain biker where the sport came of age, and Vancouver's North Shore will almost certainly enter the conversation. The dense forests of Mount Fromme, Mount Seymour and Cypress Mountain helped pioneer modern freeride mountain biking, with technical singletrack, steep descents, rock rolls and the iconic wooden bridges that have since become synonymous with the sport.

Today, the network caters to every level, from flowing beginner trails to adrenaline-spiking black diamonds, all maintained by a passionate local riding community. The payoff extends well beyond the trails themselves. Base villages and nearby neighborhoods are dotted with cafés, breweries and bike-friendly hangouts, making post-ride refueling part of the ritual. Several stops also feature on Vancouver's North Shore Ale Trail, giving riders the perfect excuse to swap helmets for tasting flights after a day in the dirt.

Whether you're chasing legendary terrain or simply curious about the birthplace of a mountain biking movement, the North Shore remains one of the world's essential riding destinations.

• Various locations

Hoop Dreams

If you happen upon the alley where Granville, Seymour, West Hastings and West Pender streets converge, you might feel like you've stepped inside a comic book—one where basketball is the main plot. *Alley-Oop* transforms an ordinary laneway into a joyful public court, splashed with a purple-and-orange mural by artist Alex Beim in collaboration with the Downtown Vancouver Business Improvement Association and HCMA Architecture + Design. It's a world away from the typical dumpster-lined back alley. If you're planning to shoot a few hoops, remember to BYOB—in this case, bring your own basketball.

- Alley-Oop, 433 Seymour Street, Downtown

Lost in the Leaves

The hedge maze at the *VanDusen Botanical Garden* is made from pyramidal cedars planted more than 40 years ago. Local legend suggests some of the gardeners never found their way out. Other than the leafy labyrinth, this oasis in the center of the city has a stone garden, sensory lab, vegetable garden and regular events to educate visitors of all ages. Think outdoor dining in partnership with local restaurants, horticultural shows led by local floral associations and art courses on botanical illustration.

- VanDusen Botanical Garden, 5251 Oak Street, Shaughnessy, vandusengarden.org

The Water Is a Playground

Vancouver is a city best experienced from the water. Framed by the Pacific Ocean, Burrard Inlet and False Creek, it offers countless ways to swap pavement for waves, whether that means paddling a kayak beneath the skyline, joining an early-morning dragon boat practice or gliding across the harbor on a stand-up paddleboard at sunset.

False Creek is especially lively in summer, with colorful ferries crisscrossing between Granville Island, Olympic Village and Yaletown. Beyond downtown, sailboats drift across English Bay beneath the North Shore mountains, while floatplanes rise from Coal Harbour, one of the world's busiest seaplane terminals, offering spectacular aerial views of the city and British Columbia's coastline. For a slower pace, hop aboard an Aquabus or False Creek Ferry, two of the city's most scenic and affordable rides.

In Vancouver, the water isn't just something to look at, it's part of everyday life. Whether commuting, exercising or soaking up the scenery, locals treat the harbor as their backyard, making it one of the defining experiences of the city.

• Various locations

A Photo Showcase by Norma Ibarra

Rolling Forward

A photographer and storyteller originally from Mexico, Norma Ibarra came to skateboarding at 31 while living near Antisocial Skateshop in Vancouver, and the sport redirected her photography entirely. Where mainstream skate media focused on professional tricks and male-dominated scenes, she turned her lens on the women, queer and BIPOC skaters who were very much part of the culture but absent from its magazines. Her work has appeared in *Thrasher* and *Vice* and in campaigns for Vans, Adidas and Nike. In 2023, Skate Like a Girl named her Lens Person of the Year.

You came to skate photography through skateboarding itself. How did becoming a skater shape the way you shoot?

I've had a camera since I was little, but photography didn't really become a job until I started skateboarding and began documenting women in the sport. I was 31 when I started skating, and it was very difficult. I kept getting hurt—broke both ankles, one year apart. I wanted to be part of the community, and I noticed that no one was documenting women who skate. I kept thinking, "How come no one is doing this?" This is history. So I started doing it myself. Before skateboarding, I was shooting mountain biking events, and that has had a huge influence on my photography. But when I got my first skate photo printed in a magazine, I was hooked.

You mention wanting to see more women in those pages, and your work extends to queer and BIPOC communities across skateboarding and action sports. Why did it feel important to you to tell these stories?

When I was young, I used to go to punk shows, and I'd see people skating, but I almost never saw women. It never felt like something that was for me. I never started until I moved to Vancouver, where the owner of the local skate shop was a woman who directed me to the women's group. I started feeling like I wanted more people like me to try it, because skateboarding had given me so much. But when you look at traditional media, the representation still isn't there. When I started, I would flip through *Thrasher* looking for women, and sometimes there were none. It's better now, but there's still no equity. I want people to be able to look at a magazine or a photo book and see themselves.

You've built long-term relationships with the people and places you photograph rather than just passing through. How do you work with your subjects, and how does that shape the work?

What's special about how I work is that I'm part of the community, not a stranger who shows up to photograph skaters. I'm a skater myself. I volunteer with nonprofits, I go to events, I show up and build relationships before I ever pick up a camera. A lot of my work started that way, shooting for the love of it because no one else was doing it. Some of my friends became professional skaters, and I was the person next to them doing the photos. It kind of became a career, but it never stopped feeling like a documentation of my life. Now that skateboarding has gone more mainstream, everyone wants to document it. But we always say: If you're not part of the community, are you telling the story the right way? That's why it matters to have more diversity behind the lens.

Skate photography has a very established visual language. How do you navigate that?

There are a lot of unspoken rules in skate photography, but I like to break them. The industry tends to be obsessed with the gnarliest trick, the historic moment, the never-been-done. I'm always asking different questions: Who's being overlooked? Who isn't being represented? I do photograph pros and sponsored riders too, but my focus is more on what we call social skateboarding: groups around the world who bring skateboarding into communities that have never had access to it. That's the part of skateboarding I love to document.

Your photobook Para Ti *was dedicated to the Mexican skate scene. How does that community compare to what you find in Toronto and Vancouver?*

Every country is different. In Mexico, there's a lot of machismo and a lack of resources, which makes it harder to be a woman in skateboarding than it already is. The social, economic and cultural dynamics add another layer of difficulty. The book is called *Para Ti*, which means "for you," because I wanted someone to pick it up and feel like it was made for them, to show them that skateboarding is for everyone. It's also the book I wish had existed when I was young. Every place you skate is going to be different, but we all speak the same language of skateboarding. You can go anywhere in the world, find a skater, and become friends. The culture of skateboarding is incredibly diverse. The industry is what isn't. For me, the work is about showing that diversity.

West Park
RESERVED
24 Hours / 7 Days
MIDLAND APPLIANCES
CUSTOMER PARKING ONLY

POSTES
CANADA

Concrete Cathedral

Set on a bluff above the Strait of Georgia at the University of British Columbia, the *Museum of Anthropology* is one of Arthur Erickson's finest buildings. Completed in 1976, it draws on the post-and-beam structure of Northwest Coast Indigenous architecture, with a low, darkened entrance that opens dramatically into the Great Hall. There, concrete columns rise 40 feet and floor-to-ceiling glass floods the space with light, framing unobstructed views of the sea. Outside, two full-scale traditional houses and totem poles built by Haida artists stand against the backdrop of the mountains and the water.

• Museum of Anthropology, 6393 Northwest Marine Drive, UBC, moa.ubc.ca

Art & Design

West Coast Canvas

Vancouver's creative spirit extends far beyond gallery walls. Discover Indigenous masterpieces, groundbreaking architecture, public art and spaces where new ideas continue to take shape.

Creative Shelter

Self-described as Canada's first Indigenous art hotel, the 18-room *Skwachàys Lodge* celebrates First Nations culture through an on-site gallery, a traditional sweat lodge, a towering rooftop totem pole and individually themed suites inspired by drum circles, forest spirits and the northern lights. More than a hotel, it's a social enterprise: Every stay supports affordable housing, studio space and professional development for Indigenous artists through an acclaimed artist-in-residence program. Housed in the former Pender Hotel, the restored building has become both a cultural landmark and a powerful example of tourism with lasting community impact.

• Skwachàys Lodge, 31 West Pender Street, Gastown, skwachays.com

Sphere of Influence

Originally built for Expo 86, the geodesic dome of *Science World* has become one of the city's most recognizable landmarks. Designed by architect Bruno Freschi, the 17-story sphere is composed of hundreds of interconnected steel triangles, following the structural principles pioneered by Buckminster Fuller. The lightweight yet remarkably strong framework creates a vast, column-free interior while maximizing natural light. By night, thousands of programmable LEDs transform the dome into a glowing centerpiece on the skyline. Once a temporary world's fair pavilion, it has endured and transformed into a major civic landmark.

• Science World, 1455 Quebec Street, False Creek, scienceworld.ca

Giants on the Waterfront

Towering over the industrial waterfront, the *OSGEMEOS Silos* are among the city's most striking public artworks. In 2014, Brazilian twin brothers Gustavo and Otavio Pandolfo, known collectively as OSGEMEOS, transformed six concrete grain silos into larger-than-life yellow characters, their dreamlike style blending folklore, fantasy and vibrant color. Painted as part of the Vancouver Biennale, the mural stretches more than 70 feet high and has become an unlikely landmark. Visible from False Creek and passing ferries, it's a vivid reminder that art can thrive in unexpected places.

• OSGEMEOS Silos, 1531 Johnston Street, Granville Island

Get Rich Art

The *Richmond Art Gallery* opened in 1980 and has operated out of the Richmond Cultural Centre since 1992, developing a curatorial program that reflects the cultural complexity of one of the most ethnically diverse areas in Canada. The permanent collection spans more than 400 works, from British Columbia landscape painters like Toni Onley and Jack Shadbolt to Indigenous artists including Bill Reid and Susan Point. The exhibition program draws on the city's position where Pacific Rim cultures converge, with a particular interest in diaspora narratives and transnational identities.

• Richmond Art Gallery, 7700 Minoru Gate, Richmond Cultural Centre, richmondartgallery.org

The Write Stuff

Artspeak is one of Vancouver's most distinctive artist-run centers, exploring visual art at the intersection of image and text. Founded in 1986, it grew out of the Kootenay School of Writing, a writer's collective rooted in language poetry and critical theory, and that literary origin has shaped its programming ever since. Small in scale but serious in ambition, it presents exhibitions by the likes of Germain Ekra (photo) alongside talks, readings and publications, consistently engaging with the political and social conditions of art-making on the West Coast.

• Artspeak, 233 Carrall Street, Gastown, artspeak.ca

Nobody Likes Me

Vancouver's most recognizable street artist is also its most elusive. Working anonymously, *iHeart* built his reputation with witty stencil works that blend humor, social commentary and digital-age satire. His viral breakthrough came in 2014 with *Nobody Likes Me*, a mural near Stanley Park depicting a distraught child lamenting a lack of Facebook likes. The work struck a nerve for its critique of social media validation. Since then, iHeart has continued to produce thought-provoking street and studio work that challenges how we interact with technology, consumer culture and one another.

• iHeart, ihatestencils.com

Rafaella Petrolacci

From Paris, with Love

Thirteen years after her move from France to Canada, the ultra-chic Rafaella Petrolacci decided to bring a bit of French style to Vancouver. Her store, *L'Appartement,* opened its doors in Kitsilano in June 2026. Kits is more known for sandals and sun hats than elevated fashion, but this shop challenges neighborhood stereotypes with clothing, shoes and accessories that are structured, refined and coveted. The small collection of styles curated by Petrolacci makes the space feel like you're stepping into someone else's home—someone with a very cool closet full of clothes they're willing to share.

L'Appartement
Kitsilano

Where did the name L'Appartement come from?

I dreamed it up as a bit of an extension of my own house. An extension of my own closet, if you will. The countertop tile is from my own kitchen. I saved it for a while and knew it would go in my store one day. Even the wallpaper—it's by Josef Frank, a midcentury Swedish designer—I've had sitting around in my house.

Are there any other significant design details in the store?

Some of the things on the wall are from my art collection, so they're pretty special. And the table is a salvaged jewelry case display that was used by a jeweler before. We cut, altered and painted it. It's beautiful and also a bit unusual.

How did you decide which brands you wanted to carry?

It's funny. People ask that question, and it's really just brands I do wear, things I've been shopping for. I'm from Paris, and every time I go back, I would just shop for my own closet. So when I had the idea for the store, I knew instinctively the brands that I wanted to bring in. Designs that I wear, but also designs that I sensed could really work here.

What do you mean by "work here"?

We live in Kits. We dress for Paris, but we still live in Kits, right? What I'm wearing today, for instance, is an outfit mostly from the brand Tinsels that I love. But I'm also wearing flats. I'm wearing stockings. I'm wearing something comfy because I run around. I

Old Faithful
Kitsilano and Gastown

Kaboodles
Kitsilano, Granville Island, Cambie Village

Parthenon
Kitsilano

Au Comptoir
Kitsilano

Folke
Kitsilano

Polygon Gallery
Lower Lonsdale

bike. I might go to the beach. I don't need a super-polished version of this outfit. You can have texture, you can have color and then you can also have total comfort.

There's definitely no shortage of texture or color. Why was this important to you?

I just want people to come in and not be bored. We all need basics, but I wanted something that is unusual, something that excites me as a shopper. When I go to stores in Paris looking for each of these brands, this is what I'm looking for. I love telling a story with color, so the store is very much organized by color.

What are your favorite brands in store?

Gas Bijoux. I feel glam without feeling decked out when I wear their jewelry, and because my mom used to wear them a lot, I am very attached to their aesthetic. There's also Tinsels, which I love because I admire their head stylist's artistry and way with color and cut. I'd also recommend Le Mont Saint Michel because their work jackets are flattering on everyone and represent so much of French heritage.

What about bags?

I'm a really big fan of bags, especially the main line that we brought in, Jack Gomme. They have this really wonderful approach to practical bags, and they like to do collaborations with artists. For example, one of their collabs with artist Marianna Ladreyt is all old materials, inflatable plastics, discarded stuff. It's really neat and almost like a piece of art around your waist.

Other than your own store, what are your favorite shops to visit in Kitsilano?

I never tire of *Old Faithful*. Their selection is pretty much flawless. I love a good toy store, so I wander into *Kaboodles* on West Broadway pretty often, with or without my son. I also visit *Parthenon* almost weekly. They have the best selection of hams and feta cheese in this part of town.

What clothing, shoes and accessories should everyone bring when visiting Vancouver?

Beyond the obvious rain gear and layering, I suggest they bring something cute that they would wear in any other city that reflects their preference, taste and culture. You don't have to leave your style at YVR. Vancouver is more than just athleisure and sporting gear, and has plenty of stylish people and venues. You just need to dare, own your style and not succumb to all yoga wear. Unless you're going to yoga, in which case, go nuts.

What are your favorite French restaurants in Vancouver?

I enjoy *Au Comptoir*'s Paris-Brest dessert and their canard confit. They're the real deal and remind me of home. And *Folke* is not French, but their tapioca dumplings are worthy of any French table.

What is one cultural attraction you think all Vancouver tourists should visit?

I don't think you can call your visit to Vancouver complete without having visited the *Polygon Gallery* on the North Shore. It's a great showcase of current Canadian art and more, an interesting building

Gatley Lifestyle Store
Grandview-Woodlands

Liberty Café
Mount Pleasant

Out and About
Gastown

The Block
Gastown

and an ambitious program. It's well worth the trip on the Seabus.

What neighborhoods should avid shoppers be sure to hit?

I would recommend exploring Main Street and Commercial Drive to get a sense of their cafés, shops and atmosphere, which are great. I especially like *Gatley [Lifestyle Store]* on Commercial for accessories, gifts and homewares, and I've been visiting *Liberty Café* on Main Street for over a decade for their scones, lattes and savory Danishes. I also recommend shopping in Gastown at *Out and About* and at *The Block* on Cordova Street, which are favorites.

Any other recommendations?

I would suggest walking in the residential neighborhoods and just having fun looking at houses. Vancouver houses run the gamut from incredibly bland to weird to extraordinary and unique, sometimes on the same block. It's always great fun to admire them and imagine who lives inside.

The Great Find

Skip the malls. The city's best shopping happens in independent bookstores, record shops and vintage boutiques, where every purchase tells a story.

Bookmark This

There's a time and a place for shopping at giant chain bookstores, but your trip to Vancouver isn't one of them. Supporting small, indie sellers is the way to go. A Chinatown standout is the beloved *Massy Books*, a Métis-owned shop that carries both current bestsellers and quirky, hard-to-find titles. Patricia Massy founded the bookstore in 2015, determined to highlight and celebrate Indigenous authors and uplift marginalized communities. The shop regularly supports those in need, and to date, has donated more than $230,000 to charities and community groups. The store often hosts book and podcast launches, readings and other cool events.

- Massy Books, 229 East Georgia Street, Chinatown, massybooks.com

Hidden Gems

It's very easy to get lost in the winding, treasure-filled labyrinth that is the historic *Mintage Mall.* Far from a warehouse-style thrift store, Mintage is located in a heritage building and consists of a series of small rooms for shoppers to peruse. The store primarily sells vintage clothing, including gently used denim, graphic tees, sports-inspired streetwear, leather jackets, retro dresses, aloha shirts and many, many boots, vests and accessories reminiscent of cowboy apparel. Welcome to the wild West Coast.

• Mintage Mall, 245 East Broadway, Mount Pleasant, mintagevintage.com

Needle Drop

Vancouver's longest-running independent record shop is also home base for one of the city's larger-than-life hometown heroes: Nardwuar the Human Serviette. The infamous YouTuber stages most of his interviews in *Neptoon*'s basement, which means Nardwuar sightings are common here. It's not impossible that you'll run into whoever he's interviewing as well. Think David Byrne, Tyler, The Creator or Prime Minister Mark Carney. The record shop itself is a crowded and vibrant maze of new and used vinyl, along with CDs, merchandise and other musical ephemera. Opened in 1981 and operated by the father-son duo Rob and Ben Frith, the shop curates a selection as good as any vinyl-loving music fanatic can ask for.

• Neptoon Records, 3561 Main Street, Mount Pleasant, neptoon.com

Read the World

More than 10 million people from all over the globe visit Granville Island annually, and for local bookseller Jennifer Kim, reflecting the neighborhood's rich cultural diversity is top of mind. The owner of *Nooroongji Books*, a multilingual independent bookstore in the island's Net Loft, offers children's picture books; language learning books for adults; and books on philosophy, art, literature and more. The name *nooroongji* comes from the Korean word for the crispy bits formed at the bottom of a rice cooker. Food, after all, is a universal language.

• Nooroongji Books, 1666 Johnston Street Unit 6, Granville Island, nooroongji.ca

The Lululegacy

There's no official uniform of Vancouver, but if there were, you can bet it would include yoga pants, sweat-wicking tops and cross-body belt bags. Get a reservation at the nicest restaurant you can find, and guaranteed there will be at least one patron wearing running shoes to dinner.

Athleisure is the name of the fashion game in this city. After all, global apparel brand *Lululemon* was founded here. Since the company started in 1998, it's grown into a multibillion-dollar business that's changed the way people dress both inside Vancouver and out. Smaller activewear brands like *Londre*, *DAUB* and *LEZÉ the Label* are carrying the torch forward with a focus on ethical and sustainable manufacturing as well as comfort. And while plenty of Vancouverites are mostly practicing the "leisure" part of athleisure, just as many are putting their movement-ready clothing to the test on the daily, participating in indoor cycling classes at *Spin Society*, Pilates at spots like *Lagree West*, boxing at gyms like *Rumble*, and, of course, yoga at studios like *YYOGA*.

You can't blame Vancouverites for going straight from HIIT class to happy hour. That's what the uniform is for.

• Various locations

Be an elite diner
Earn 2X points on gas station, grocery store and dining purchases
The Air Canada Aeroplan® Card
Experience something elite.
Learn more at
Chase.com/AirCanadaCard
AIR CANADA
AEROPLAN
CHASE
Mastercard, the circles design, World Mastercard and World Elite Mastercard are trademarks of Mastercard International Incorporated. Chase Air Canada Aeroplan Card credit cards are issued by JPMorgan Chase Bank, N.A. Member FDIC. Accounts subject to credit approval. Restrictions and limitations apply. Offer subject to change.

James Priestner

Rare Americans, Real Vancouver

Rare Americans has carved out a unique place in modern music, pairing cinematic storytelling with animated videos that have attracted hundreds of millions of views online. Frontman James Priestner (middle in photo) reflects on the band's unconventional rise and offers an insider's guide to the local scene, from iconic music studios and venues to great food, craft beer and winter fun.

HippoSonic Recording Studio
Mount Pleasant

The Warehouse Studio
Gastown

You often pair your music with animation. Was that the vision from the beginning?

I was producing videos and TV commercials for different companies, and we knew from the very beginning that we wanted a very strong visual component. We wanted to go directly to YouTube first as totally independent. We knew storytelling was a big part of the songs, so we made several music videos for the first album. Six of them were live action, and one was an animated video. It just so happened that people really connected with the animated video.

For our second album, we commissioned three more as animated. One of them went ultra viral with almost 100 million views on YouTube, and the other two went kind of viral as well. The music entertainment field is dominated by a strong front person taking up 90 percent of the screen, and this seemed like a niche that not a lot of artists were doing. There's the Gorillaz, who are at the top of the mountain, but besides that, we felt we had an open lane.

For someone who is not familiar with your work, which video should they check out first?

The *Brittle Bones Nicky* series. We did parts one, two and three, so it's almost like a short film, and the series has as much popularity as our band. People always ask for a *Brittle Bones Nicky* movie because they really connect with the characters. But the project I'm the most proud of is a punk rock animated musical called *(S)KiDS* that's based on a true story.

Do you perform live with the animation?

We usually try to have video. Sometimes people get too sucked into the video and almost forget that we are there on stage. Then when we try no video, you see people are more engaged with you. So it's always a hybrid where it's not just full-blown animation. But, the short answer is yes, we do usually incorporate video.

Does a YouTube hit translate to traditional radio spins?

Radio has never been our lane. We've really tried to build out the animated universe so people start to identify with these characters and the problems and the hardships they have in life. For a lot of artists, it's so different, and radio was the path you needed to get there. Now it's about virality, whether it's TikTok or whatever, and YouTube has been our discovery platform for the most part.

In a lot of ways, it's decentralized the music industry.

Exactly, but it also makes it harder. Now there are 120,000 songs being uploaded every day to Spotify. Trying to stand out in the crowd has never been more challenging, but it does give a 17-year-old kid in their room an equal shot.

Tell me about the iconic recording studios in Vancouver.

The most famous is *Little Mountain Sound Studios*, which recorded Aerosmith, Bon Jovi, Metallica, AC/DC, Kiss. It's now *HippoSonic*, but the original live room is still there, and you see pictures of rock legends all over the walls. We've recorded several albums there. *The Warehouse [Studio]* is the other famous one, which is owned by Bryan Adams, who got his start here in Vancouver. It's probably the most state-of-the-art recording studio that we have, and the legends of

The Commodore
Granville Entertainment District

Vogue Theatre
Granville Entertainment District

the legends have been there. He built it in Gastown, which is like the original frontier of Vancouver. It's a gritty part of town but very cool. It feels very European.

Artists often start or end tours in Vancouver, so you might go near the studio, and there will be tons of Suburbans and security, and then you'll catch wind that Eminem was doing some tour prep there. We've also recorded there. It's a very beautiful room.

I was surprised to learn that Bob Rock started here. He produced some classics: Metallica's Black Album, *the Cult's* Sonic Temple, *Mötley Crüe's* Dr. Feelgood.

He was like the house engineer at Little Mountain Sound. When you're young, you just cut your teeth on anything you can possibly find. You're just getting the reps in, and sure enough, it happens that you're dealing with a very talented human being. Pretty soon, you make one great record, and people want to work with you.

Say you want to do a big concert. Where would you play in Vancouver?

The Commodore is probably the legendary spot. We actually have two venues on the same street, the other being the *Vogue Theatre*, which both have about a thousand cap[acity]. It's like they directly compete against each other.

I remember seeing Tate McRae play at the Vogue Theatre for a thousand people about three years ago. Artists, especially international ones, often only hit two cities in Canada, usually Toronto and Vancouver, so we get almost every

Fortune Sound Club
Chinatown

Tavola
West End

Maenam
Kitsilano

Torafuku
Chinatown

artist on their major international tours. So any artist who's playing in an arena now probably played at the Commodore or the Vogue Theatre first.

What about a venue that holds 75 to 150 people?

Fortune Sound Club in Chinatown has been around for a really long time, and it's just around the corner from The Warehouse Studio. You'll see someone play there on their very first tour, and then the next tour they're probably gonna be at the Commodore. You can see artists at Fortune that are eventually gonna upstream to the bigger venues.

Any emerging local bands or artists you like right now?

Fionn are twin sisters on a local label called 604 Records founded by Nickelback's Chad Kroeger with Jonathan Simkin. The label had a breakout smash with "Call Me Maybe" by Carly Rae Jepsen, and it continues to support local artists. The Jins is another, and they're eerily similar to Nirvana. The lead singer looks and sounds like Kurt Cobain.

What are some of your favorite restaurants?

Tavola has always been one of my favorites. It's an Italian restaurant that makes everything from scratch daily, and there's a fresh board because the restaurant is plugged into the local farmer scene. *Maenam* is a Thai restaurant in Kitsilano, which is a very cool part of the city. It's a small restaurant, so it can be hard to get into, but every bite is going to be a 10 out of 10. *Torafuku*

Steamworks
Various locations

Granville Island Brewing
Fairview

Brassneck Brewery
Mount Pleasant

Red Truck
Mount Pleasant

Strange Fellows
Strathcona

Stanley Park
West End

Pacific Spirit Park
Point Grey

Crystal Mall
Burnaby

Richmond Night Market
Richmond

Granville Island
Fairview

Shipyards District
Lower Lonsdale

Time Out Market
Oakridge

is incredibly creative. You go into this place, and you don't really know what to expect. It's like they have shared picnic table seating, and the chef is a mastermind.

What about drinks?

We have a craft beer scene similar to Seattle and Portland. *Steamworks* is my favorite. *Granville Island Brewing* and *Brassneck Brewery* are also super good. *Red Truck*, *Strange Fellows*. Many of the breweries also serve pizza, and they're concentrated in a couple areas, so people rent bikes and do little brewery tours.

What about hiking or biking trails?

Vancouver excels at this more than any city I've ever been to around the world. They could have sold off so much of the real estate, but they deliberately kept it as green space, which makes the city what it is.

The seawall is number one, and it connects the downtown core. You can almost do a full circle that goes through *Stanley Park*, which is bigger than Central Park [in NYC]. It's a rainforest, and you can bike or walk all the way around it. You can also see whales, seals, bald eagles.

Number two, *Pacific Spirit Park*, which has 70 kilometers of trails. They have beautiful off-leash parks there, and the dogs can go swimming right on the beach.

I live in the North Shore, and this is the entry point to Squamish and Whistler. We have the Capilano River Valley with endless trails here. A black bear has literally visited my yard three times this week, which is a little bit concerning, but that's the beauty of living on the North Shore. You're really immersed in nature.

Burnaby nearby has the Crystal Mall with food stalls like you would find at a hawker market in Singapore. There are probably 50 different stalls with vendors hand-pressing dumplings, hand-pulling noodles or making fresh soups. All the signs are in Chinese, with no English whatsoever, and it's cash only. *Richmond Night Market* is another one.

Any other recommendations?

Granville Island is a must. You have local farmers selling fresh produce and a big food court and a ton of small independent artisan stores selling everything from ceramic mugs to beautiful paintings. Then you have the *Shipyards District*, or the Lonsdale Quay, which is like the North Shore's answer to Granville Island. We also have the *Time Out Market*.

Outside of skiing and snowboarding, what is the must-do activity in the winter?

Honestly, my answer would not really change. You just have to be prepared for cloudiness and rain. We go through long stretches in the winter where the rain can last two straight weeks, and I'm not joking. Those periods can be challenging, but the food scene is still going to be awesome. You still have amazing concerts, and you can go to a Vancouver Canucks game or on a nice walk. It's temperate here, so it's not going to be minus 20 like the rest of Canada. Just come prepared with umbrellas and rain gear.

CHEEZ-IT

Hot Ticket

In 1906, the building at the corner of East Cordova and Gore was home to one of Vancouver's first fire stations. Now it's home to a striking performing arts theatre. *Firehall Arts Centre* stages live musicals, plays, concerts and dance shows that spotlight both local and international talent in a truly one-of-a-kind venue. Yearly events include the Dancing on the Edge Festival, the country's longest-running contemporary dance festival. Check online for upcoming events.

• Firehall Arts Centre, 280 East Cordova Street, Railtown, firehallartscentre.ca

Culture

Off Script

From punk pioneers and comedic rebels to stage shows and film shoots, the creative scene has always moshed to its own beat.

BC Punk

Music historians typically focus on Hermosa Beach, Berkeley and San Fran when discussing the early roots of West Coast punk, but Vancouver has a legacy that at least deserves a seat at the table. By the late 1970s, the short-lived The Skulls gave way to D.O.A. and Subhumans, while D.O.A. drummer Chuck Biscuits went on to play with Black Flag, Circle Jerks, Social Distortion and Danzig (immediately after The Misfits). Along with other early acts like Braineaters, Young Canadians and Pointed Sticks, the scene punched far above its weight and even popularized the term "hardcore" with D.O.A.'s *Hardcore 81* album.

Photo: Sarah Race

A Higher Calling

Long before cannabis was legal in Canada, Cheech and Chong were turning it into comedy gold. The counterculture duo—Cheech Marin and Tommy Chong, who was born in Edmonton and raised in Calgary before launching his career in Vancouver—got their start performing in the city's nightclub scene during the late 1960s. Their laid-back humor, absurd sketches and cult films went on to influence generations of comedians, making Vancouver an unlikely birthplace for one of comedy's most iconic double acts. A fitting piece of local trivia before lighting up—legally, of course.

Laugh Riot

Less than a 10-minute walk from Waterfront Station is *Little Mountain Gallery*, an indie hub for stand-up, sketch and improv comedy. The small but mighty space has two stages, one upstairs and one down, and is artfully decorated with neon signs and stuffed raccoons (a tribute to the very real animals that once burdened the original venue). LMG is the place to see the wacky, weird and wonderful humor of Vancouver, from your standard stand-up format to a musical karaoke parody show featuring owl puppets.

• Little Mountain Gallery, 110 Water Street, Gastown, littlemountaingallery.ca

Scene Stealer

Vancouver's Rise as a Filmmaking Powerhouse

If the Oscar for Best Actor could be awarded to a city, Vancouver would win in a landslide. For decades, the city has been one of Hollywood's most versatile stars, effortlessly transforming into American cities and towns, remote wilderness and even entirely fictional worlds. Vancouver has played a leading role in hundreds of beloved films and television series, earning its well-deserved nickname: Hollywood North.

The credits are staggering. Comedies like *Happy Gilmore, Juno, Elf* and *Hot Tub Time Machine* were filmed here, alongside blockbusters including *Deadpool, X-Men, Mission: Impossible—Ghost Protocol, Twilight, Godzilla* and *Fifty Shades of Grey,* among others. *First Blood,* the 1982 hit that launched the Rambo franchise, stands out as one of the earliest major local productions, filmed just east of Vancouver in the Fraser Valley.

Television has an equally rich history in the city. *MacGyver* and Johnny Depp's *21 Jump Street* were among the earliest American network series filmed in Vancouver, but it was *The X-Files* that helped establish Vancouver as a premier production hub. During its formative seasons in the 1990s, the series leaned into the region's misty forests, dramatic bridges and overcast skies to create its unforgettable atmosphere. Since then, countless series—including *Supernatural, Riverdale, Fringe, Once Upon a Time, The Flash* and *Yellowjackets*—have relied on the city's remarkable ability to become almost anywhere.

But Vancouver is much more than a convincing stand-in. Beyond the sound stages and blockbuster productions, it has cultivated a thriving independent film community, with local writers, directors and actors helping shape Canadian cinema. The beloved *Rio Theatre* hosts cult classics, Canadian premieres, filmmaker Q&As and themed movie nights, while the *VIFF Centre* screens an outstanding year-round program of international and homegrown films. Every autumn, the *Vancouver International Film Festival* brings acclaimed filmmakers and cinephiles from around the world to the city, celebrating the creativity that makes Vancouver not just a backdrop, but one of North America's great filmmaking capitals.

All You Can Feast

One of Vancouver's most anticipated annual summer festivals is *Brewery and the Beast.* This single-day event brings together the best restaurants and bars in the city for an outdoor smorgasbord of barbecue heaven. Thanks to more than 80 vendors, this festival is the place for Wagyu steak, tacos, waffles, chicken wings, personal apple pies and more all on the same day. It's the fastest and most thorough "greatest hits" of the dining scene you can hope to get. Sorry, vegans: This event is extremely meat-heavy.

- Brewery and the Beast, Concord Pacific Place, 88 Pacific Boulevard, Downtown, breweryandthebeast.com

Gather

Join the Crowd

The best way to get to know Vancouver? Show up. These outdoor feasts, art crawls and street parties give visitors a reason to join the celebration.

Open Invitation

Hosting pop-up dance parties in unconventional spaces is the name of the game for *Public Disco,* a decade-old nonprofit dedicated to fun, inclusive, music-centered events. This might look like a daytime DJ set outside a local café, a pride party in a renovated motel courtyard, or an all-vinyl open-air dance floor set up at the *Vancouver Art Gallery.* Or it could be cherry-blossom-themed block parties, all-ages functions perfect for families and even free events that you might discover by chance. Just watch for the people dancing in the streets.

- Public Disco, various locations, publicdisco.ca

Festive Fear Factor

At any time of year, the 450-foot-long pedestrian suspension bridge crossing the North Shore's Capilano River can put your heart in your throat. Even those who claim no fear of heights cower when swaying more than 200 feet above the ground. But during the holiday season, beautiful lights transform the bridge and surrounding evergreen trees, making it the holliest, jolliest adrenaline rush around. This attraction is outside the city of Vancouver itself, but a free shuttle regularly runs back and forth between downtown and the bridge. The journey takes about 20 minutes, depending on traffic.

- Capilano Suspension Bridge, 3735 Capilano Road, North Vancouver, capbridge.com

Reel Summer Nights

When the sun goes down, Stanley Park becomes Vancouver's largest open-air cinema. Held every Tuesday evening during the summer, *Evo Summer Cinema* transforms the Ceperley Meadow lawn into a giant outdoor screening room, with blockbuster favorites and cult classics projected beneath the stars. Bring a blanket, pack a picnic or pick up snacks on-site, then settle in as the mountains fade into silhouettes behind the screen. Arrive early to claim a good spot. The atmosphere is as much a part of the experience as the film itself, making it one of the city's best-loved summer traditions.

• Evo Summer Cinema, Grand Lawn at Ceperley Meadow in Stanley Park, summercinema.ca

Underground Art

The work of some artists is impossible to miss. Think Yue Minjun, whose iconic *A-maze-ing Laughter* sculptures have become a symbol of the West End, or Myfanwy MacLeod, who created the towering sparrows of *The Birds* in Olympic Village. Others work beyond the public eye, exhibiting in artist-run centers, alternative galleries and experimental spaces. Each October, the Vancouver *Outsider Arts Festival* celebrates creators who are self-taught, have experienced social exclusion or work outside the traditional art world. It's one of the city's best places to discover an artist you'll be talking about long before everyone else catches on.

• Vancouver Outsider Arts Festival, 181 Roundhouse Mews, Yaletown, voaf.ca

Twinkling Treetops

There's something heartwarming about wandering through a forest of trees shining bright with holiday lights. The hot chocolate and a bag full of piping-hot mini donuts help, of course. From late November through early January, *VanDusen Botanical Garden* gets a merry makeover with more than a million artfully placed lights. There are mesmerizing light tunnels, interactive exhibits and regularly scheduled light shows that bring the garden to life with a gorgeous audiovisual display. The garden is open no matter the weather, so dress extra-warm on frosty days.

- VanDusen Festival of Lights, 5251 Oak Street, Shaughnessy, vandusengarden.org

Open Studios

Across four days each November, Eastside Arts Society organizes a self-guided tour through the historic Strathcona neighborhood—one of the oldest in the city, and one of the most culturally vibrant. Art studios dominate the neighborhood, with many of the artists living in these spaces. People are invited in to get a sense of what the artistic community is actually like while soaking up the history of one of Vancouver's original neighborhoods, where Chinese migrants and local timber workers once lived, worked and played. It's a heady, gorgeous trip down the city's past and into its eclectic artistic heart.

- Eastside Culture Crawl, Strathcona, culturecrawl.ca

Get lost in the right places
OPEN
Off the map, but in your feed. Follow for hard-to-find recommendations.

Explore

Vancouver

Your Next Great Escape

In most cities, you spend the day moving from one landmark to the next. In Vancouver, you can go from a downtown café to the deep wilderness before lunch. When it comes to Canada's west coast, the best adventures here aren't found on a checklist of museums and monuments, but on the water, high in the mountains and across rainforest trails. The only question is which one you'll tackle first.

Stanley Park

Sunset Beach

Great adventures demand great fuel, so stock up on trail snacks first. When you use your Chase Air Canada Aeroplan® Card, you'll earn 2X points on grocery store purchases. Once packed, head to Stanley Park for an easy introduction to the city's wild side. The sprawling urban oasis occupies a forested peninsula just off downtown, with hiking trails, seawall paths and panoramic views across the water. Prefer a higher vantage point? Visit Queen Elizabeth Park, the highest point in the city, to take in landscaped gardens, sweeping views and a cascading waterfall in the Quarry Garden.

On your first full morning, it's time to choose your element. If you prefer the water, rent a kayak or paddleboard and explore False Creek or Burrard Inlet, where snowcapped peaks rise behind downtown towers and curious harbor seals occasionally pop up to say hello. Early risers can join a local dragon boat session, while sun-seekers can head to Kitsilano Beach or Sunset Beach to catch a Pacific sunset.

For an adventure on two wheels, cross the inlet to the North Shore, where mountain-bike trails thread through the forested slopes of Mount Fromme, Mount Seymour and Cypress Mountain. Widely regarded as the birthplace of modern freeride mountain biking, the region offers everything from technical rock rolls and steep descents to more forgiving routes for beginners. The North Shore also boasts exceptional hiking trails in places like Capilano Suspension Bridge Park. Afterward, follow the North Shore Ale Trail and reward yourself with a pint of craft beer, earning 2X points at restaurants when you pay with your card.

If alpine terrain is calling, hop in a car and take the iconic Sea-to-Sky Highway north. As a cardmember, you can enjoy 2X points on gas and a fourth night free at 300,000+ hotels worldwide. In warmer months, Garibaldi Provincial Park becomes a hiker's paradise with turquoise lakes, lush meadows and dramatic viewpoints like Panorama Ridge.

Stanley Park

Whether you tackle one element or all of them, every point earned on groceries, gas, dining and travel can bring you that much closer to your next getaway. With the Chase Air Canada Card, you'll earn 5X total points on eligible Air Canada purchases and receive up to $100 in Air Canada statement credits annually. Plus, you'll enjoy automatic Elite Status with no minimum spending requirement, unlocking benefits like Priority Check-In, free first checked bags and Priority Boarding (Zone 2) for a more seamless travel experience. This card is available exclusively to qualified individuals with a U.S. address.

Already thinking about your next adventure? With Air Canada's 180+ destinations and over 1,300 destinations across its 45+ global airline partners, returning to the mountains or escaping to the ocean is easier than ever.

Scan or learn more at chase.com/aircanadacard

Editors' Picks

The BC Canon

Get Hazy

Heading home with local craft beer? Start the shopping list with Colour & Shape, a hazy IPA from *Superflux Beer Company.* With tropical fruit, citrus and soft stone-fruit flavors, the award-winning beer balances a pillowy mouthfeel with restrained bitterness.

- Colour & Shape, superfluxbeer.com

Pour It On

Mẹ's Nuoŭớc Mắm (Mom's Fish Sauce) brings the family recipe from Anh and Chi restaurant to your kitchen. Made locally in Vancouver, this award-winning condiment balances rich umami, tangy sweetness and a gentle chile kick. Use it as a dipping sauce, dressing, marinade or finishing splash for everything from grilled meats to noodle bowls.

- Mom's Fish Sauce, anhandchi.com/products

Living Threads

Rain Goose Textiles reimagines Coast Salish weaving traditions through contemporary blankets, scarves and home goods by Coast Salish artist and designer Melaney Gleeson-Lyall. Crafted from ethically sourced natural fibers, each piece reflects the landscapes and living traditions of the Salish Sea.

- Rain Goose Textiles, raingoose.com

Sweet Peaks

Cast in molds inspired by local mountain peaks, *Polygon Bars* deliver small-batch chocolate filled with inventive flavors like London Fog, Cookie Monster and Pop Rocks. They're proof that chocolate can be equal parts dessert and edible art.

- Polygon Bars, shop.beta5chocolates.com

Read

Vancouver Photographs
• Fred Herzog, 2007

Fred Herzog documented everyday life in Vancouver from the 1950s onward, helping pioneer the artistic use of color and street photography. His vivid images of neon signs, storefronts and ordinary people have become an enduring visual record of the city's postwar transformation. Published as part of a major 2007 retrospective at the Vancouver Art Gallery, the book and show brought Herzog the international acclaim his work had long deserved.

Stanley Park
• Timothy Taylor, 2001

When chef Jeremy Papier opens his dream restaurant, he finds himself caught between the high-stakes world of local food trends and a decades-old mystery buried deep within Stanley Park. Part culinary drama, part Pacific Northwest noir, Taylor's debut novel paints a vivid portrait of a city caught between its wild roots and global ambitions.

The Jade Peony
• Wayson Choy, 1995

Set in Chinatown during the 1930s and 1940s, this acclaimed novel follows a Chinese Canadian family through the eyes of three siblings, each navigating the tensions between tradition and belonging in a changing city. Rich in memory and detail, it's celebrated for its exploration of immigration, identity and the resilience that helped shape Vancouver's multicultural roots.

Watch

Everything's Gone Green
• Paul Fox, 2006

This offbeat comedy follows a disillusioned slacker lured into a world of easy money, lottery winners and shady schemes. Cannabis grow-ops, real estate dreams and a golf course designer all color this sharp portrait of Vancouver, fittingly written by the Canadian novelist who popularized the term "Generation X."

Double Happiness
• Mina Shum, 1994

Long before *Grey's Anatomy* and *Killing Eve*, Sandra Oh delivered her breakout performance as an aspiring actress torn between her family's traditional expectations and her own dreams. Recognized as the first feature by a Chinese Canadian woman to receive a wide theatrical release in Canada, Mina Shum's acclaimed debut captures the complexities of identity and multicultural Vancouver with warmth and wit.

Hard Core Logo
• Bruce McDonald, 1996

This cult mockumentary follows a fictional Vancouver punk band on one last reunion tour across Western Canada. While often compared to *This Is Spinal Tap*, it trades broad satire for a darker story of friendship, ambition and disillusionment. Headstones frontman Hugh Dillon stars as the band's volatile lead singer, with a soundtrack that features punk legends like the Ramones, D.O.A. and Teenage Head.

Spin

"Assimilate"
• Skinny Puppy, 1985

"Assimilate" is a defining Skinny Puppy track and a landmark of early industrial music. Released in 1985, the track delivers pounding electronics, distorted vocals and an unsettling atmosphere that helped shape the genre worldwide. Dark, confrontational and innovative, the song captures the experimental spirit that made Vancouver an unlikely hub for electronic music.

"Home for a Rest"
• Spirit of the West, 1990

Kudos to Canada for turning a miserable hangover lament into the country's unofficial drinking anthem. Powered by Celtic-inspired melodies and a sing-along chorus, the 1990 hit remains a pub favorite that now celebrates hard living and harder partying. Many travelers can relate, so if you hear it in a Canadian bar, grab a pint and join the chorus. You'll sound like a local.

"Kaputt"
• Destroyer, 2011

Indie icons Destroyer reached new heights with "Kaputt," the title track from an album that made year-end best-of lists by *Rolling Stone* and *NME*. Blending sophisti-pop, jazz and dreamlike lyrics, the song swaps indie rock grit for shimmering saxophones and lush melodies. Elegant and enigmatic, it cemented Destroyer as one of Canada's most acclaimed art-pop acts.